I LOVE BACKPACKING THE WEST

Carole Ayres

©2018 Carole Ayres. All rights reserved.
This work is protected by the copyright laws of the United States of America. No part of this book may be reproduced or stored, in whole or in part, in print or digital format, without express permission by the author. For information regarding permission, interviews, events, and quotes, write to the publisher:

Crippled Beagle Publishing, dyer.cbpublishing@gmail.com
Photo credits: Carole Ayres and Joe Ayres
Book design by Jody Dyer
Scriptures taken from American King James Version and Berean Study Bible
ISBN-13: 978-1970037-09-08

I LOVE BACKPACKING THE WEST

Carole Ayres

"The Lord shall preserve your going out and your coming in from this time forth, and even for ever more." —Psalm 121:8 (AKJV)

For my grandchildren.

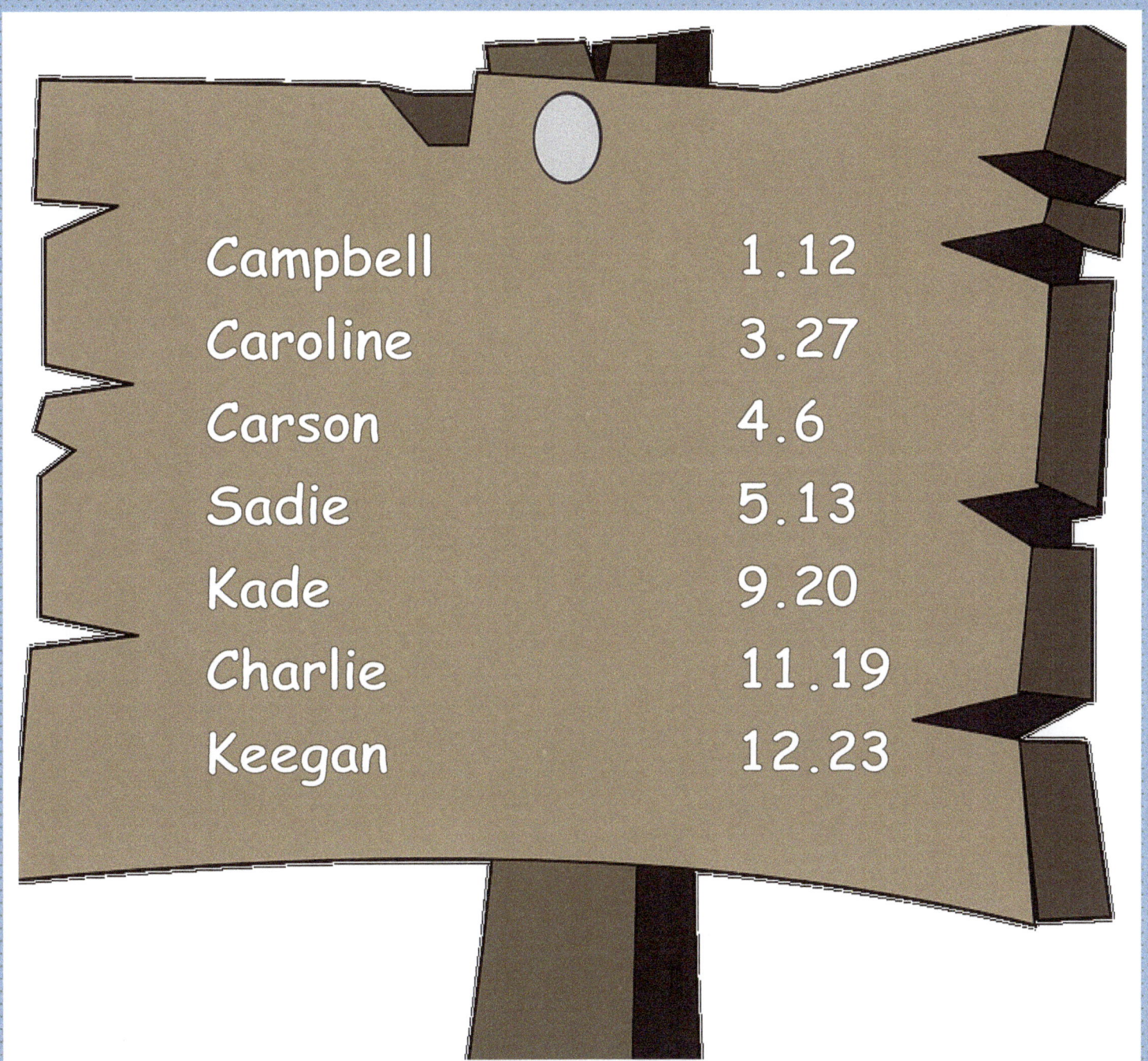

Campbell	1.12
Caroline	3.27
Carson	4.6
Sadie	5.13
Kade	9.20
Charlie	11.19
Keegan	12.23

Packing List

- sleeping bags
- food
- flashlights
- sturdy shoes
- food
- rainfly
- water purifier
- compass
- flashlights
- sunscreen
- sunglasses
- trekking Poles
- headlamp
- transponder/phone
- toiletries
- shovel
- tent
- fishing gear
- clothes
- mess kit
- cooking supplies
- first aid kit
- map
- bug spray
- bear whistle
- hats
- camera
- lighter/matches
- sleeping pad
- knife
- jacket
- hang bag

This is what it looks like to go backpacking out West.
Magnificent scenery God made for us to see and to test.

The West has very high mountains and beautiful lakes.
A backpack full of food, gear, and clothes is all it takes.

Walking all day makes you want to stop and rest.
Even on the side of a cliff, because the view is the best.

Lie on your back, turn your face to the sun.
Listen to the wind, your nap has just begun.

Once we finish dinner, to the lake we go.

Wash the dishes. Hurry! The nights beginning to show.

As we watch the night draw near,
we close everything up tight.
We enjoy each other's company,
then crawl into our tents for the night.
In the morning we will linger, our heads still full of rest.
Let's go see Yellowstone National Park.
We know we'll all be impressed.

In Yellowstone Park we watch Old Faithful shoot high.
How do people know when and where it's headed to the sky?
The earth knows the timing,
God set it all in place.
Rangers tell us when to watch.
Only earth knows the pace.

Next we'll go to see the forest
that burned down a few years back.
Now it's growing quickly and it's back on track.

In Montana, Glacier Park is where we'll go.
We head to Going to the Sun Road,
which often has lots of snow.
Right next to the road is this giant waterfall.
Everyone stops to watch. Eyes open wide with awe.

Maybe it takes more than food and clothes to backpack way out West.

Backpacking takes an adventurous spirit, too.
Also a compass and strong legs to find the view.

Dear reader I hope you can someday
go see the beauty of God's world out West.
And I hope you stay to play.

"A man's heart plans his course, but the Lord determines his steps."

—Proverbs 16:9 (BSB)

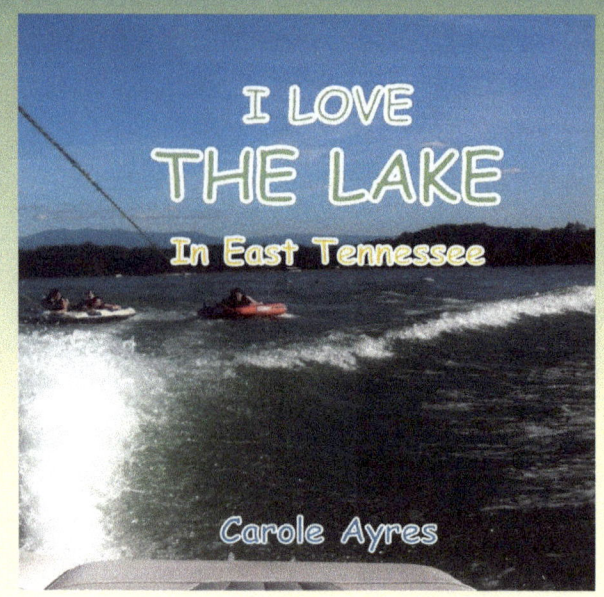
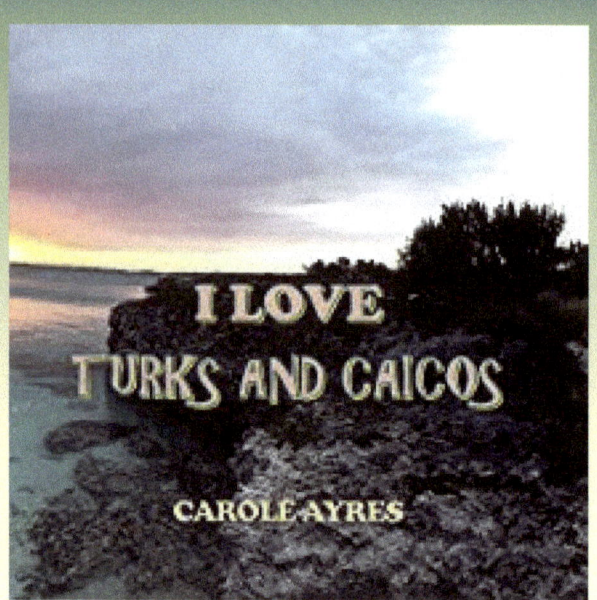

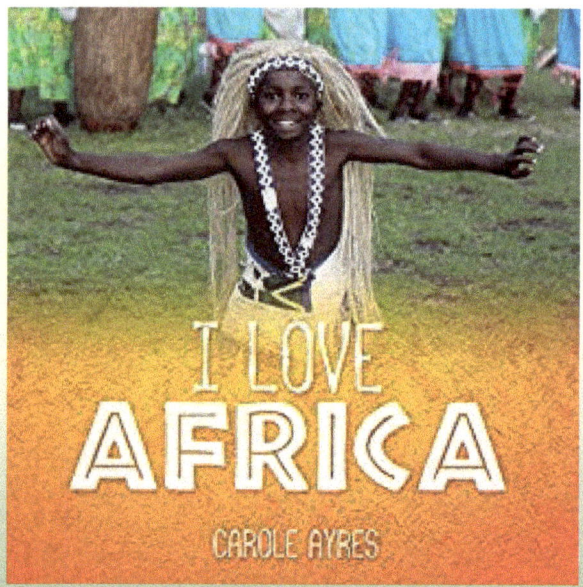

About the Author

Carole Ayres lives in Tennessee with her husband Joe. She is a retired teacher who travels the world. When she is home, Carole tutors young people and spends time serving her church and playing outdoors with her grandchildren.

Look for other *I LOVE* books by Carole Ayres on Amazon.com, Kindle, and at a variety of retailers. For information on future titles, book signings, and interviews, write to:

Crippled Beagle Publishing, 5413 Glen Cove Drive
Knoxville, Tennessee 37919
dyer.cbpublishing@gmail.com